Presidential Passages

The Use Of The Bible In Presidential Inaugurations

Ken Kettlewell

Fairway Press, Lima, Ohio

PRESIDENTIAL PASSAGES

Copyright © 2004 by
Fairway Press
Lima, Ohio

Scripture quotations marked (KJV) are from the *King James Version of the Bible,* in the public domain.

All photographs in this book were taken by Ken Kettlewell.

Library of Congress Control Number: 2004109297

ISBN 0-7880-2125-7   PRINTED IN THE U.S.A.

ACKNOWLEDGMENTS

Jim Bohren, Heritage Presbyterian Church, Centerville, Ohio, for his suggestion of the name for this book while I was Interim Minister of that congregation.

Burton Public Library, Detroit, Michigan, where I did beginning exploration of the subject of this book.

PREVIOUS BOOKS PUBLISHED BY KEN KETTLEWELL

Your Ethical Compass
(Sermons on the Ten Commandments)
Express Press, Lima, Ohio, 1989

Our Town: New Concord
(Hometown of John Glenn)
Express Press, Lima, Ohio, 2001

White House Portico

INTRODUCTION

Every four years, the person whom we have elected to serve for four years as "The President of the United States" takes an oath, with millions of us watching on television and thousands of spectators present in Washington, D.C.

The first presidential inauguration I remember was in 1937 (FDR's third) when our school teacher, Paul M. Davis, took us to his home to listen to the ceremony on the radio. Mrs. Davis served us cookies. I don't remember the inaugural address. I do remember the cookies.

The first presidential inauguration I remember on television was Harry S. Truman's in 1948. My wife and I went to the home of a parishioner, Martha Pye, to sit in front of her television. I remember watching the dignitaries coming in and taking their places on the platform.

As we watch an inauguration, we observe a Bible. How does it come that the Bible, consisting of the Old and New Testaments, plays a part in the Inauguration of the President of the United States? Does the Constitution prescribe the left hand be placed on a Bible and the right hand be raised while the oath is being taken? Does the Constitution specify that the Bible be opened to a particular page or passage?

"No" to both questions. The Constitution is silent on the matter. There is no detail at all for the ceremony except these words of the oath: "I do solemnly swear (or affirm) that I will faithfully execute the office of President of the United States and will to the best of my ability preserve, protect and defend the Constitution of the United States."

Dating all the way back to our first president, the use of the Bible is purely traditional. Ever since George Washington, a Bible has been used at all the inaugurations except for that of John Quincy Adams, as the reader will learn when coming to his page. Many, not all, have directed that the Bible be opened to a particular passage. Sometimes, the Bible is opened at random; sometimes it has remained closed.

A bit of confusion surrounds the use of the Bible in inaugurations, along with much error. (This would be a good time for me to admit that errors will probably appear here and there along the way in this book.) One columnist a few years ago said, "No two presidents have been sworn with the same passage." Reading this book, you will see this is not so.

Correspondence with presidential libraries has been interesting and helpful. One librarian suggested that perhaps Congress has kept all the inaugural Bibles, stored carefully among archival treasures. That isn't the way of it, either.

I have long been intrigued by two simple questions: 1) What Bible was used? 2) If opened, to what passage was it open?

These two questions I try to answer for the reader. The research has taken me to books, newspapers, magazine articles, speeches, correspondence. The reports do not always agree, in which case I have attempted to present the various possibilities.

Home of George and Martha Washington
Mount Vernon, Virginia

Tomb of our first president,
Mount Vernon, Virginia

Above the entrance are these words of Jesus:
"Whosoever liveth and believeth in me shall never die"
— John 11:26.

Our 1st President:

George Washington

two terms

Thursday, April 30, 1789,
on the balcony of Federal Hall in New York City
and
Monday, March 4, 1793

"It is impossible to rightly govern the world without God and the Bible."[1]

George Washington took his oath of office as the first president of the United States on the altar Bible of Saint John's Masonic Lodge No. 1, New York City.[2] The red velvet cushion on which it rested was also brought from the Lodge. Boller writes, "The Bible was a last minute acquisition."[3]

Chancellor Robert R. Livingston, Grand Master of Masons in New York State, called on Major Jacob Morton, Washington's Aide and Marshall of the day, to produce the Lodge Bible for the occasion. Morton was the Master of Saint John's Lodge, No. 1, the oldest Masonic Lodge in the city.

The Bible was opened to the 49th chapter of Genesis, the first book in the Bible.[4] (Some say it was opened at random.)

After taking the oath, Washington leaned over and kissed the Bible, after which the crowd broke into a chant: "Long live George Washington, president of the United States." A memorial leaf of the Bible was then folded at this page. Joseph Morton (Master of St. John's Lodge) stepped forward and turned down the corner.

The King James version Bible, included the Apocrypha and maps. It was printed in London by Mark Baskett, "printer to the King, 1767." It was presented to the Lodge by Jonathan Hampton on November 28, 1770, the night Hampton was elected Master of Saint John's Lodge. The story of Washington's use of the Bible in his inauguration is recorded on one of the flyleaves.

The same Bible was carried by the Lodge in the procession in New York on December 31, 1799, when Washington died; also on February 21, 1885, at the dedication of the Washington Monument in Washington, D.C. It continues to be in active use in the Saint John's Lodge.

We note in connection with the Masonic Bible that George Washington was Worshipful Master of his Lodge of Freemasons in Alexandria, Virginia. Installed in 1788, he continued in that office for twenty months. He wore his Masonic apron when he laid the cornerstone of the Capitol, that apron having been given to him by Madame Lafayette.

Washington's second Inaugural was held on Monday, March 4, 1793, in the Senate Chamber of Congress Hall in Philadelphia. What Bible was used in the ceremony is declared unknown.

"The George Washington Inaugural Bible" has been used in five other Presidential Inaugurations, each time at the request of the new president: Zachary Taylor, Warren G. Harding, Dwight D. Eisenhower, Jimmy Carter, George H. W. Bush.

The committee from Saint John's Lodge No. 1 in New York City was invited to the White House the morning of the inauguration of George H. W. Bush. One of the members recalls that Barbara Bush asked, before the ceremony, if she might hold the "Washington Bible" to see how heavy it was, for she would be holding it in the ceremony.[5]

It was almost used in the Inauguration of George W. Bush in 2001. A committee of three from Saint John's Lodge brought it to Washington, D.C., by train.[6] Paul Magnotta, one of the three, was serving as Master of the Lodge. Due to the cold, damp weather, it was decided at the last minute to use another Bible.

A treasure in the Saint John's Lodge, the "George Washington Masonic Bible" is on public display in a Plexiglas case, at Federal Hall in New York City. Special lighting and atmospheric control assure its permanent care. The pages in Genesis to which it was opened are covered with silk, which is almost invisible to the eye.

Comment on the passage (Genesis 49) to which the Bible was opened:

We can only conjecture the reason for the Bible being opened to this passage. George Washington may well have been thinking of the thirteen colonies which made up this new nation called "The United States of America." Even as Jacob blessed the twelve tribes, so Washington was praying for God's blessing to be upon each of the thirteen colonies. If indeed the Bible was deliberately opened to the book of Genesis, how appropriate, the beginning book of the Bible for the beginning of this new nation.

1. National Bible Association, <httpᐟ/www.nationalbible.org/>
2. Boudreau, Dr. Allan, *The Northern Light,* "Washington Bible — Afterthought Or Planned?" (Scottish Rite Northern Masonic Jurisdiction) May, 1989.
3. Boller, Paul F., Jr., *Presidential Inaugurations* (Orlando, Florida: Harcourt, Inc., 2001), p. 12.
4. Historical pages from Saint John's Masonic Lodge No. 1, New York City.
5. Conversation with Most Worshipful John C. Mountain, Saint John's Lodge No. 1, 9-11-03.
6. Curtis, Richard H., editor, *The Northern Light,* "Footnotes" (Scottish Rite Northern Masonic Jurisdiction) May, 2001.

We have little or no information on the use of the Bible in the inaugurations of the presidents from John Adams through John Tyler.

Our 2nd President:

John Adams

one term

"Suppose a nation in some distant region should take the Bible for their only law book, and every member should relegate his conduct by the precepts there contained! Every member would be obliged in conscience to temperance, frugality and industry: to justice, kindness and charity towards his fellow man: and to peity, love and reverence toward Almighty God ... What a Utopia, what a Paradise would this region be."[1]

1. Errant Skeptics Research Institute <http://www.errantskeptics.org/ Quotes_by_Presidents.htm> [1999] John Adams Diary, February 22, 1756.

Monticello, home of Thomas Jefferson
Charlottesville, Virginia

Our 3rd President:

Thomas Jefferson

two terms

**Wednesday, March 4, 1801
and
Monday, March 4, 1805**

"I have always said and always will say that the studious perusal of the Sacred Volume will make better citizens, better fathers, and better husbands ... the Bible makes the best people in the world."[1]

1. Errant Skeptics Research Institute <http://www.errantskeptics.org/Quotes_by_Presidents.htm> [1999].

Our 4th President:

James Madison

two terms

Saturday March 4, 1809
and
Thursday, March 4, 1813

"We have staked the whole future of our new nation not upon the power of government; far from it. We have staked the future of our political constitution upon the capacity of each of ourselves to govern ourselves according to the moral principles of the Ten Commandments." [1]

"Even church state separationist took his oath on a Bible." [2]

1. Errant Skeptics Research Institute <http://www.errantskeptics.org/Quotes_by_Presidents.htm> [1999].
2. Boller, Paul F., Jr. *Presidential Inaugurations* (Orlando, Florida: Harcourt, Inc., 2001), p. 129.

Tomb of President James Monroe
Richmond, Virginia

Our 5th President:

James Monroe

two terms

Tuesday, March 4, 1817
and
Monday, March 4, 1821

"The liberty, prosperity, and the happiness of our country will always be the object of my most fervent prayers to the Supreme Author of All Good."[1]

1. Errant Skeptics Research Institute <http://www.errantskeptics.org/ Quotes_by_Presidents.htm> [March 5, 1821 — Second Inaugural Address].

Our 6th President:

John Quincy Adams

one term

Friday, March 4, 1825

"So great is my veneration for the Bible, that the earlier my children begin to read it, the more confident will be my hope that they will prove useful citizens to their country and respectable members of society."[1]

Comment:

Such a quotation is not surprising from a man whose daily practice was to read two chapters of the Bible.[2]

The only president not to use a Bible in the Inauguration ceremony, the new president swore allegiance on a book containing the laws of the U.S.A. Mr. Adams was "no conventional secularist" but his conscientiousness about reserving the Good Book for strictly religious purposes was "unique." He also omitted "So help me God." Franklin Delano Roosevelt also omitted those four words, but all others have added them.[3]

1. National Bible Society, Comments about the Bible, John Quincy Adams.
2. Kittler, Glenn D., *Hail To The Chief,* "The Inauguration Days Of Our Presidents," Philadelphia, Pennsylvania: Chilton Book Company, 1965, p. 35.
3. *Ibid.*, p. 40.

Tomb of President Andrew Jackson at his home,
"The Heritage," near Nashville, Tennessee

Our 7th President:

Andrew Jackson

two terms

Wednesday, March 4, 1829
and
Monday, March 4, 1833

"The Bible is the Rock which this Republic rests."[1]

Chief Justice Marshall met Jackson in front of a table covered with a scarlet cloth on which the Bible lay. After taking his oath, the new President picked up the Bible, kissed it, and replaced it.[2]

---

1. Errant Skeptics Research Institute <http://www.errantskeptics.org/Quotes_by_Presidents.htm>.
2. Boller, Paul F., Jr., *Presidential Inaugurations* (Orlando, Florida: Harcourt, Inc., 2001), p. 129.

Our 8th President:

Martin Van Buren

one term

Monday, March 4, 1837

Mr. Van Buren quoted the Bible in his Inaugural address.

> *"May her ways be ways of pleasantness and all
> her paths be peace."*[1]   — Proverbs 3:17

After taking the oath, he kissed the Bible.[2]

1. Presidential Inaugurations: Bibles and Scripture Passages,
   <http:memory.loc.gov/ammem/pihtml/pibible.html>.
2. Kittler, Glenn D., *Hail To The Chief,* "The Inauguration Days Of Our Presidents," Philadelphia, Pennsylvania: Chilton Book Company, 1965, p. 45.

Our 9th President:
William Henry Harrison

one term

Thursday, March 4, 1841

After he entered the White House, Mr. Harrison purchased a Bible and a hymnbook and read them daily until his death one month later.[1]

1. Kittler, Glenn D., *Hail To The Chief,* "The Inauguration Days Of Our Presidents," Philadelphia, Pennsylvania: Chilton Book Company, 1965, p. 54.

Tomb of President John Tyler
Richmond, Virginia

Our 10th President:

John Tyler

one term

Tuesday, April 6, 1841

Our 11th President:

James Knox Polk

one term

Tuesday, March 4, 1845

The Bible was printed at Oxford by the University Press in 1841. On several blank pages in the front of the volume, there is a letter addressed to Mrs. Polk. Signed by Alexander Hunter, Marshal of the District of Columbia, it notes that the Bible was presented to Mrs. Polk. It is now in the possession of the James Knox Polk Memorial Auxiliary, Columbia, Tennessee.[1]

"The oath taken, he kissed the Bible."[2]

1. Rare Book Library, Cathedral of Saint Peter and Saint Paul, Washington, D.C.
2. Kittler, Glenn D., *Hail To The Chief,* "The Inauguration Days Of Our Presidents," Philadelphia, Pennsylvania: Chilton Book Company, 1965, p. 58.

Tomb of President Zachary Taylor
Louisville, Kentucky

Our 12th President:

Zachary Taylor

one term

Monday, March 4, 1849

"It was for the love of the truths of the great and good book that our fathers abandoned their native shores for the wilderness."[1]

His daughter wrote: "My father was a constant reader of the Bible, and practiced all its precepts, acknowledging his responsibility to God."[2]

George Washington was Mr. Polk's hero, and now following him into the White House, he used the Bible George Washington had used. The new president's hand rested on it. After taking the oath, he kissed the Bible.[3]

1. Villefuere, Nelly F., *A Charm Offensive,* No. 2, under "Zachary Taylor, Bible Quote."
2. *Ibid.*
3. Kittler, Glenn D., *Hail To The Chief,* "The Inauguration Days Of Our Presidents," Philadelphia, Pennsylvania: Chilton Book Company, 1965, p. 63.

Our 13th President:
Millard Fillmore

one term

Wednesday, July 10, 1850

*"I shall place my confidence in God and in the
Bible. I rely upon Him who holds in His hands the
destinies of nations to endow me with the requisite
strength for the task, and to avert our country from
the evils apprehended from the calamity that has
befallen us."*[1]

A Bible, a hymnbook, an almanac, and an occasional newspaper were all in the Fillmore home library. Mr. Fillmore had committed many verses and chapters of the Bible to memory.[2]

1. American Bible Society, 1865 Broadway, New York, New York 10025.
2. Kittler, Glenn D., *Hail To The Chief,* "The Inauguration Days Of Our Presidents," Philadelphia, Pennsylvania: Chilton Book Company, 1965, p. 68.

Our 14th President:

Franklin Pierce

one term

Friday, March 4, 1853

"Over fifty years ago, I began reading the Bible. Immediately, I began learning exciting new truths."[1]

Chief Justice Taney held the closed Bible while Mr. Pierce put his left hand on it and raised his right. He did not kiss the Bible.[2]

But according to the following story, there was no Bible at the Pierce Inauguration:

A tragedy had befallen Mr. and Mrs. Pierce weeks before the Inauguration. On January 6, 1853, they and their small son, Bennie, boarded the train in Boston for Concord, New Hampshire. Along the way, there was a sudden jolt and the car they were sitting in slipped off the track, toppled off the embankment, and rolled into a field. Mr. Pierce and his wife were slightly injured, but Bennie was caught in the wreckage and crushed before their eyes.

The Pierces never fully recovered from the disaster. They asked themselves if God was punishing them because they had failed to honor Him rightly. Mrs. Pierce finally decided that God had taken Bennie so her husband would have no family distractions to take him away from his presidential responsibilities.

But Pierce himself continued to interpret the loss as punishment for his sins, and as a result, he refrained from using the Bible at his Inauguration.[3]

Instead, he broke precedence by raising his right hand and affirming rather than swearing his loyalty to the United States Constitution. He was the only one to "affirm."

1. American Bible Society, 1865 Broadway, New York, New York 10025
2. Kittler, Glenn D., *Hail To The Chief,* "The Inauguration Days Of Our Presidents," Philadelphia, Pennsylvania: Chilton Book Company, 1965, p. 73.
3. Boller, Paul F., Jr., *Presidential Anecdotes,* p. 115.

Our 15th President:

James Buchanan

one term

Wednesday, March 4, 1857

"I may say that for twelve years I have been in the habit of reading the Bible and praying every day."[1]

The Bible used by James Buchanan, printed in Oxford by the University Press in 1853, contains an inscription signed by William T. Carroll, Clerk of the Supreme Court, on the back flyleaf attesting to its use at the Inauguration. It belongs to the National Museum of American Art at the Smithsonian Institution, but is on indefinite loan to the National Museum of American History.[2]

---

1. *Positive Atheists, Big List of Quotations*, No. 1 under "James Buchanan, Bible Quotes."
2. Letter to Dr. W. M. Paxton, pastor of First Presbyterian Church, New York City, President James Buchanan.

Lincoln, "Uncle Sam," and Washington
scene created for a display in the
First Presbyterian Church, Detroit, Michigan, 1975

Our 16th President:
Abraham Lincoln

two terms

Monday, March 4, 1861

"I believe the Bible is the best gift God has ever given to man. All the good ... of the world is communicated to us through this book."[1]

In 1864, Mr. Lincoln wrote to his friend, Joshua Speed: "Take all of this Book that you can on reason, and the rest on faith, and you will live and die a better man."[2]

Presiding for the ceremony was Chief Justice Roger Brooke Taney, his ninth and last time to preside at a Presidential Inauguration.

After taking the oath, Mr. Lincoln bent and kissed the Bible. There are conflicting accounts of whether the Bible was open and if open, whether at random or a chosen passage. The Bible is almost identical to Buchanan's, containing a similar inscription signed by William Thomas Carroll, Clerk of the Supreme Court. It is in the Library of Congress.

March 4, 1865

This was the occasion of Lincoln's wonderful second Inaugural address which included the line:

"With malice toward none; with charity for all; ..."

The whereabouts of the 1865 Bible are not known. Among the Robert Todd Lincoln papers in the Library of Congress Manuscript Division is a letter from Chief Justice Chase transmitted to Mrs. Lincoln. It includes a specific account: "The Bible kissed by your honored husband, on taking today, for the second time, the oath of office as President of the United States." Again, there are conflicting accounts whether the Bible was open or not. Perhaps it was opened to one of these three verses:[3]

> *"Judge not that ye be not judged."*
> — Matthew 7:1

> *"Woe unto the world because of occasions of stumbling."*
> — Matthew 18:7

> *"Yea, O Lord God, the Almighty, true and righteous are thy judgments."*
> — Revelation 16:7

Comment on the Passages in Matthew and Revelation to which the Bible was opened:

The judgment of Almighty God weighed heavily on Lincoln's heart. He had a profound sensitivity to an understanding that our thoughts, our actions, our very lives are all under the judgment of God. One thinks of the line in "Mine Eyes Have Seen the Glory" which we sing: "He is sorting out the hearts of men before His judgment seat." It is said that when President Lincoln first heard this hymn by Julia Ward Howe, he had tears in his eyes. So do we as we sing that glorious hymn.

1. Carl Sandburg's Introduction of *Lincoln Devotional*. Greatneck, New York: Channel Press, 1957, p. x.
2. *Ibid*, p. xvi.
3. Curator, Architect of the Capitol, President Abraham Lincoln.

The Lincoln Memorial
Washington, D.C.

Our 17th President:

Andrew Johnson

one term

Saturday, April 15, 1865
the morning of Lincoln's death

Within an hour after receiving word of his predecessor's death, Mr. Johnson replied: "I am ready."[1]

Placing his hand on the open Bible, Mr. Johnson took his solemn oath. The ceremony was held in the parlor of Kirkwood Hotel.

What Bible was used? There are two reports, in conflict. The first by Chief Justice John Wright: The Bible was printed in Philadelphia by E. H. Butler and Co., 1864. Its whereabouts are unknown.[2]

The second: The Cathedral exhibition catalog describes it as printed at Cambridge by the University Press, in 1859, with the inscription: "Andrew Johnson's Inaugural Bible. When oath was taken his hand rested on Chapters 20 and 21 on the front inside board."[3]

> *"Kindness and truth preserve the king."*
> — Proverbs 20:28

> *"Every way of a man is right in his own eyes; but Jehovah weigheth the hearts."* — Proverbs 21:2

The same Bible may have also been used on March 4, 1865, when Mr. Johnson was sworn in as Vice President. It is kept in the custody of the National Park Service.

According to the Cathedral exhibition catalog, yet another Bible (New York, American Bible Society, 1856) is in the hands of an unidentified owner. It contains a note: "The manuscript authentication of Owen Rogers Stafford, son of a witness of the Inaugural ceremony in the lobby of the Kirkwood Hotel on April 15, 1865. The Bible had been fetched by his father for Johnson's use on that occasion."[4]

Comment on the passage (Proverbs 20, 21) to which the Bible was opened:

The book of Proverbs in the Old Testament includes a wealth of wisdom, verse after verse, chapter after chapter. Billy Graham once said to a group of ministers in Cleveland: "Every month, I read through the 31 chapters of Proverbs, a day at a time." These two verses are well worth remembering for a president or for anyone of us. Kindness and truth should be our intention. And what is important is not what seems right in our eyes, but what is right in God's sight.

1. Kittler, Glenn D., *Hail To The Chief,* "The Inauguration Days Of Our Presidents," Philadelphia, Pennsylvania: Chilton Book Company, 1965, p. 94.
2. Rare Book Library, Cathedral of Saint Peter and Saint Paul, Washington, D.C.
3. *Ibid.*
4. *Ibid.*

Our 18th President:

Ulysses S. Grant

two terms

Thursday, March 4, 1869

"Hold fast to the Bible as the sheet-anchor of your liberties. Write its precepts on your heart and practice them in your lives. To the influence of this book we are indebted for all the progress of civilization, and to this we must look as our guide in the future."[1]

Perhaps the Bible was open to Isaiah 10:1-3:[2]

"Woe to unjust judges and to those who issue unfair laws, says the Lord. So that there is no justice for the poor, the widows and orphans. Yes, it is true that they even rob the widows and fatherless children. O what will you do when I visit you in that day when I send desolation upon you from a distant land?"

General Grant used a Bible in 1869, but no information about it is available. After taking the oath of office, he kissed the Bible.[3]

Comment on the verses (Isaiah 10:1-3) to which the Bible may have been opened:

It would seem that President Grant had a profound sensitivity to injustice. Along with that sensitivity, he must have had a fear of the day when the Lord would send desolation upon a people who mistreat the poor, the widows, the orphans. We are reminded of Julia Ward Howe's words in "Mine Eyes Have Seen the Glory," "He is trampling out the grapes of wrath before His judgment seat."

Tuesday, March 4, 1873

The Senate Sergeant-at-arms opened a Bible at random. Some sources say it was opened to Isaiah 11:2. "And the spirit of the Lord shall rest upon him: the spirit of wisdom and understanding, the spirit of counsel and insight, the spirit of knowledge and of the fear of the Lord."[4]

After President Grant took his oath of office for a second time, the Bible was passed to Chief Justice Chase who held it up for the President to kiss.[5]

The Bible was printed in London by Eyre and Spottiswoode (no date). Owned by the Chicago Historical Society, it contains a certificate signed by D. W. Middleton, Clerk of the Supreme Court.[6]

Comment on the verse (Isaiah 11:2) to which the Bible may have been opened:

This verse comes from the very next chapter in Isaiah, following the verse which may have been chosen for the first inauguration. The prophet speaks of the coming Messiah and how "the Spirit of wisdom and knowledge and the fear of the Lord" will rest upon Him. It would seem that President Grant hoped that that same Spirit might rest upon him. A worthy wish as he entered his second term of office.

1. Halley, *Bible Handbook*, p. 18.
2. Rare Book Library, Cathedral of Saint Peter and Saint Paul, Washington, D.C.
3. Kittler, Glenn D., *Hail To The Chief,* "The Inauguration Days Of Our Presidents," Philadelphia, Pennsylvania: Chilton Book Company, 1965, p. 101.
4. Presidential Inaugurations: Bibles and Scripture Passages, <http://memory.loc.gov/ammem/pihtml/pibible.html>.
5. Architect of the Capitol, files compiled by the Office of the Curator.
6. Rare Book Library, Cathedral of Saint Peter and Saint Paul, Washington, D.C.

Our 19th President:

Rutherford Birchard Hayes

one term

Monday, March 5, 1877

March 4 came on Sunday, and Mr. Hayes preferred the ceremony be postponed until Monday. With the permission of President Grant, a private ceremony was held on Saturday, March 3, when Rutherford B. Hayes took the oath of office. Hayes stated, "I did not altogether approve, but acquiesced."[1]

Concerning the Chief Clerk of the Supreme Court, James H. McKenney wrote: "Clerk Middleton, my predecessor, held the Bible when Hayes took the oath. He marked the Bible with a lead pencil and later I took it to the White House to read to Mrs. Hayes. Mrs. Hayes laughed and said that President Hayes was too kindhearted to destroy anything."[2]

The passage was Psalm 118:12: "They swarm around me like bees; but in the name of the Lord I cut them off."

The Bible, printed in London by Eyre and Spottiswoode, is in the Rutherford B. Hayes Library at Fremont, Ohio.[3]

Comment on the verse (Psalm 118:2) to which the Bible was open:

We don't know, but perhaps the "bees" had swarmed around Mr. Hayes until he grew weary of them during the campaign. Everyone running for president has all sorts of accusations to contend with, all sorts of challenges. It must be most wearing to go through a political campaign such as every president goes through. Perhaps Mr. Hayes' choice of verses was a humorous response to the "bees" which not only buzzed, but stung him. If that is the way of it, he was not overwhelmed. He had not let them get the best of him. If that is the way it was, we are glad for that!

1. Williams, Charles R., *Diary and Letters of Rutherford Birchard Hayes*, Vol., p. 426.
2. *New York Times,* March 4, 1905, p. 2.
3. Rare Book Library, Cathedral of Saint Peter and Saint Paul, Washington, D.C.

Our 20th President:

James A. Garfield

one term

Friday, March 4, 1881

The Bible was open to Proverbs 21:1 "The king's heart is in the hand of the Lord; as the rivers of water, he turneth it whithersoever he will."[1]

After Chief Justice Waite administered the oath, Mr. Garfield kissed the Bible, then his mother, then his wife.[2]

The Bible was printed at Oxford by the University Press, and according to the Washington Cathedral cataloger, it is one of the finest of the Oxford editions used for Presidential Inaugurations. A certification of its use was inscribed and signed by James H. McKenney, Clerk of the Supreme Court. It is owned by the Lake County Historical Society, Mentor, Ohio.[4]

Comment on the verse (Proverbs 21:1) to which the Bible was opened:

Who is in charge of your life and mine? Are we in charge? Do we feel strong enough, wise enough, astute enough to be in charge? Or, down deep, would we really want to let God be in charge? In His infinite ways, He knows what is best. This verse in Proverbs is saying that the king (or the president) is in a good situation if his heart is in the hand of the Lord, for the Lord can, and will, direct him just as He directs the way a river goes.

1. Presidential Inaugurations: Bibles and Scripture Passages,<http://memory.loc.gov/ammem/pihtml/pibible.html>.
2. Kittler, Glenn D., *Hail To The Chief,* "The Inauguration Days Of Our Presidents," Philadelphia, Pennsylvania: Chilton Book Company, 1965, p. 112.
3. Architect of the Capitol, files of the Office of the Curator.
4. Rare Book Library, Cathedral of Saint Peter and Saint Paul, Washington, D.C.

Our 21st President:

Chester Alan Arthur

one term

Tuesday, September 20, 1881, in New York City

Mr. Arthur first took the presidential oath in New York City, at his private residence. A drawing by J. W. Alexander shows a closed Bible with Judge Brady holding it with his left hand while Mr. Arthur clasps it in his left hand.[1]

The Bible used in this first oath-taking ceremony was printed in Philadelphia by J. B. Lippencott, 1857, and it is now in a collection in the Library of Congress.[2]

Thursday, September 22, 1881, in Washington, D.C.

The Bible used on this occasion was printed in London by Eyre and Spottiswoode (no date) and contains McKenney's certification. In 1969, it was in the possession of Mr. Charles Pinkerton, Mount Kisco, New York.[3]

Presiding in the ceremony was Chief Justice Waite. Supreme Clerk McKenney opened the Bible he was carrying to Psalm 31:1-3. "In thee, O Lord, do I take refuge. Let me never be put to shame. Deliver me in Thy righteousness. Thou art my rock and my fortress." After taking the oath, Mr. Arthur kissed the Bible.[4]

Comment on the verses (Psalm 31:1-3) to which the Bible was opened:

"In God We Trust" appears on our coins. President Arthur was expressing his personal trust in God. He was offering this humble prayer of the Psalmist that he might be delivered from wrong. He trusted God to protect him and keep him from wrong choices which would bring shame upon his name and his administration. What a fine prayer to offer!

1. Collections of the Library of Congress.
2. Rare Book Library, Cathedral of Saint Peter and Saint Paul, Washington, D.C.
3. *Ibid.*
4. Kittler, Glenn D., *Hail To The Chief,* "The Inauguration Days Of Our Presidents," Philadelphia, Pennsylvania: Chilton Book Company, 1965, p. 117.

Our 22nd President:

Grover Cleveland

one term

Wednesday, March 4, 1885

*"I don't believe, as a people, that we can afford to
allow our interest in and veneration for the Bible
to abate."*[1]

The Bible used was a small edition which his mother had given
him when he was fifteen years old, published in New York by the
American Bible Society in 1851. Certifications by the Supreme
Court Clerk, Mr. McKenney, appear on two blank leaves in the
front. In 1969, it was owned by Richard F. Cleveland, Baltimore,
Maryland.[2]

Well worn, the Bible had been on Mr. Cleveland's desk in every office he had held. Having taken the oath, the new President
kissed it and slipped it into his pocket.[3]

The Bible was opened by Chief Justice, at random, to Psalm
112:4-10:[4] "All goes well for the generous man who conducts his
business fairly. Such a man will not be overthrown by evil circum-
stances. God's constant care of him will make a deep impression
on all who see it. He does not fear bad news, nor live in dread of
what may happen. For he is settled in his mind that the Lord will
take care of him. That is why he is not afraid, but can calmly face
his foes. He gives generously to those in need. His deeds will never
be forgotten. He shall have influence and honor. Evil-minded men
will be infuriated when they see all this. They will gnash their teeth
in anger and slink away. Their hopes are thwarted."

Comment on the verses (Psalm 112:4-10) to which the Bible was opened:

If the Bible was opened at random, indeed it was a propitious place! The Psalmist speaks of the blessings which come to the person who is generous and fair. God's constant care will be with him. He won't live in fear of bad news. He knows in his heart that God will take care of him. His influence will continue after he is gone. His deeds will be remembered.

Anyone who gains the Presidency will surely hope and pray for all this is to be true, in as great a degree as possible.

1. American Bible Society, 1865 Broadway, New York, New York 10025.
2. Rare Book Library, Cathedral of Saint Peter and Saint Paul, Washington, D.C.
3. Kittler, Glenn D., *Hail To The Chief,* "The Inauguration Days Of Our Presidents," Philadelphia, Pennsylvania: Chilton Book Company, 1965, p. 117.
4. Presidential Inaugurations: Bibles and Scripture Passages, <http://memory.loc.gov/ammem/pihtml/pibible.html>.

Tomb of President Benjamin Harrison
Crown Point Cemetery, Indianapolis, Indiana

Our 23rd President:

Benjamin Harrison

one term

Monday, March 4, 1889

*"There are some things we cannot dispense with
and among them are God's Word and Truth and
those influences by which He brings the heart of
man into subjection to moral law."* [1]

The Bible used for the oath taking was one printed in Oxford
by the University Press (no date). It contains Clerk McKenney's
certification. It is owned by the President Benjamin Harrison Foun-
dation, Inc., in Indianapolis, Indiana.

The Bible belonged to the Harrison family and was brought
from Indianapolis for the occasion. "General Harrison removed
his hat as he held the Bible and then raised it to his lips." Most of
the gathered crowd held umbrellas in the heavy rain. They could
hardly hear the ceremony or see because of the rain. But when the
new President kissed the Bible, they knew the oath had indeed
been taken. [2]

The Bible was opened to Psalm 121: [3] "I will lift up mine eyes
unto the hills; whence cometh my help? My help cometh from the
Lord who made heaven and earth ... The Lord shall keep thy going
out and thy coming in from this time forth and forevermore."

Comment on the passage (Psalm 121) to which the Bible was opened:

The 121st Psalm has often been called "The Traveler's Psalm."
It might well be the daily prayer of all of us. Our help does come
from the Lord, and the Lord does watch over us as we enter into
projects and as we finish them, as we come and as we go. It would
seem that President Harrison was putting his trust in the Lord to
guide him in his presidency.

1. Rare Book Library, Cathedral of Saint Peter and Saint Paul, Washington, D.C.
2. *Ibid.*
3. Presidential Inaugurations: Bibles and Scripture Passages. <http://
memory.loc.gov/ammem/pihtml/pibible.html>.

The flag of the United States of America
drapes Hudson's Department Store in Detroit, Michigan, on
Flag Day, June 4, 1973.

Our 24th President:

Grover Cleveland

one term

Wednesday, March 4, 1893
his second inaugural

The Bible was opened to Psalm 91:12-16: "They shall bear thee up in their hands, lest thou dash thy foot against a stone. Thou shalt tread upon the lion and adder. The young lion and the serpent shalt thou trample under foot. Because he hath set his love upon me, therefore will I deliver him. I will be with him in trouble. I will deliver him and honor him. With long life will I satisfy him, and show him my salvation."[1]

Chief Justice Waite administered the oath of office. A young man holding a small morocco-covered, gilt-edged Bible presented it. President Cleveland raised the Bible to his lips after taking the oath.

James H. McKenney, Clerk of Supreme Court, reported: "He was the owner of a small Bible, not larger than our hand. His mother had presented it to him when he was a boy, and he had treasured it ever since. It was used at both Inaugurals."[2]

Comment on the passage (Psalm 91) to which the Bible was open:

Interesting choice of passages for a president on his inauguration day! Was Mr. Cleveland feeling that trouble might lie ahead of him? Big troubles? Lions and serpents? Not knowing what was ahead, as no human can know, he was expressing his faith that the Lord's love would surround him and deliver him through whatever might be his lot.

1. Presidential Inaugurations: Bibles and Scripture Passages,<http://memory.loc.gov/ammem/pihtml/pibible.html>.
2. *New York Times,* February 14, 1909, p. 10, col. 6.

Our 25th President:

William McKinley

two terms

Thursday, March 4, 1897

*"The more profoundly we study this wonderful
Book, and the more closely we observe its divine
precepts, the better citizens we will become and
the higher will be our destiny as a nation."*[1]

When the time came for the oath to be taken, Marshal
McKenney of the Supreme Court lifted the large and ornate Bible,
and the new President bowed and kissed it.[2]

The Bible was presented to Mr. McKinley by Bishop Arnett of
Wilberforce College, near Xenia, Ohio. Its covers were of blue
morocco with satin lining, white satin panels, and gilt edges. A
gold plate in the center of the cover was engraved: "William
McKinley, President of the United States of America, inaugurated
March 4, 1897."

The Bible, published in Cincinnati by the Western Methodist
Book Concern, in 1896, was a gift to the President from the bish-
ops of the African Methodist Episcopal Church. It contains a certification signed by Chief Justice Melville W. Fuller. In 1969 it was
in the possession of the Reverend William McKinley Duncan,
Camden, Arkansas.

The Bible was opened to 2 Chronicles 1:10: "Now give me
wisdom and understanding to rule them properly for who is able to
govern by himself such a great nation as this?"[3]

Comment on the verse (2 Chronicles 1:10) to which the Bible was opened:

President McKinley chose to have the Bible opened to the prayer King Solomon offered after the Lord had said to him: "Ask what I shall give you." The one thing above all else that Solomon wanted was wisdom and understanding. Recognizing the huge responsibility which was upon him to govern a nation, Solomon knew what he needed most was wisdom and understanding.

President McKinley identified with King Solomon in this humble prayer. What a wonderful attitude for a person beginning his administration!

Monday, March 4, 1901

The Bible was opened for this Inauguration to Proverbs 16:20-21: "He that giveth heed unto the word shall find good; And whoso trusteth in the Lord, happy is he. The wise in heart shall be called prudent. And the sweetness of the lips increaseth learning."[4]

The 1901 Inaugural Bible, was printed in Oxford by the University Press, 1896. It also is certified by Chief Justice Fuller. It is in the collections of the Western Reserve Historical Society, Cleveland, Ohio.[5]

Comment on the verse (Proverbs 16:20-21) to which the Bible was opened:

A member of the Methodist Church in Canton, Ohio, William McKinley was married to Ida Saxton in Christ Presbyterian Church, Canton. He recognized the wisdom presented in the book of Proverbs in the Old Testament. He would begin his second presidential term trusting God to give him wisdom and guidance, recognizing that therein would lie his happiness.

1. National Bible Association, Comments About The Bible, William McKinley.
2. *New York Times,* March 5, 1897.
3. Clerk of the Supreme Court, 1939, list compiled.
4. Presidential Inaugurations: Bibles and Scripture Passages, <http://memory.loc.gov/ammem/pihtml/pibible.html>.
5. Rare Book Library, Cathedral of Saint Peter and Saint Paul, Washington, D.C.

Our 26th President:

Theodore Roosevelt

two terms

Tuesday, September 4, 1901

"Almost every man who has by his lifework added to the sum of human achievement has based his life work largely upon the teachings of the Bible."[1]

Mr. Ansley Wilcox, at whose home, the ceremony was held, wrote in 1903: "According to my best recollection, no Bible was used, but President Roosevelt was sworn in with uplifted hand."[2] Federal District Judge John R. Hazel administered the oath.

Saturday, March 4, 1905

Theodore Roosevelt used a Bible on this occasion printed in Oxford by the University Press (no date) upon which he had been sworn in as Governor of New York in 1898. It contains Chief Justice Fuller's certification. In 1969, it was owned by Theodore Roosevelt, III, Philadelphia, Pennsylvania.[3] After taking the oath, President Roosevelt kissed the page in the open Bible.[4]

The Bible was opened to James 1:22. "Be doers of the word and not hearers only."[5]

Comment on the verse (James 1:22) to which the Bible was opened:

This verse is a good one for any one of us to keep before us at all times in life. We are to "be doers" and not just "hearers." That is, we are to hear and then do something about what we have heard. The Bible is full of good counsel. It isn't enough to read it or listen to the minister preach about it. We are to put the good counsel into action. We are to live the word.

Great verse that Theodore Roosevelt chose!

54

1. Theodore Roosevelt.
2. *Ibid.*
3. Rare Book Library, Cathedral of Saint Peter and Saint Paul, Washington, D.C.
4. Kittler, Glenn D., *Hail To The Chief,* "The Inauguration Days Of Our Presidents," Philadelphia, Pennsylvania: Chilton Book Company, 1965, p. 147.
5. Presidential Inaugurations: Bible and Scripture Passages, <http://memory.loc.gov/ammem/pihtml/pibible.html>.

Birthplace of William Howard Taft
2038 Auburn Avenue
Cincinnati, Ohio

Jean Kettlewell standing at the entrance

Our 27th President:

William Howard Taft

one term

Thursday, March 4, 1909

In the days before the ceremony, many offers of Bibles were made.[1] There was actually little debate, however. Chief Justice Melville Fuller brought the century-old Bible from the Supreme Court to the ceremony. It contains his certification concerning the oath-taking. There was deep touch sentiment in the use of this Bible, for the new President's oath for the Supreme Court was taken on this same book, as it was also for new members of the court for generations.[1]

It was on this same Bible that President Taft took his oath in 1909, that his great grandson, Bob Taft, took his oath of office as Governor of the State of Ohio in 1999, and again in 2003, in Columbus, Ohio.

The Bible was opened to 1 Kings 3:9. "Give therefore thy servant an understanding heart to judge thy people, that I may discern between good and evil; for who is able to judge this great people?"[2]

Following the oath, President Taft took the Bible in both hands and kissed it. This act of reverence by the Unitarian brought a gasp of satisfaction from the gallery, climaxed by a thunderous applause.[3]

An 1888 edition, Oxford University, the Bible was owned by Charles P. Taft, Cincinnati, in 1969.

Comment on the verse (1 Kings 3:9) to which the Bible was opened:

Called in the Children's Catechism "the wisest man," Solomon went, early in his reign, to Gilboa to offer sacrifices to God. God appeared to him in a dream one night. God was saying to Solomon: "Ask what I shall give you."

This verse is Solomon's response to God's offer. Solomon's request pleased the Lord. God said to Solomon: "Because you have not asked for long life, neither for riches, nor the life of your enemies ... I have given you an understanding heart, so that there has been none like you before you, neither after you shall any arise like unto you."

What a wonderful choice, among all the verses in the Bible, for the new President on his day of oath-taking!

1. *New York Times,* March 14, 1909, p. 2.
2. Presidential Passages: Bibles and Scripture Passages, <http://memory.loc.gov/ammem/pihtml/pibible.html>.
3. Kittler, Glenn D., *Hail To The Chief,* "The Inauguration Days Of Our Presidents," Philadelphia, Pennsylvania: Chilton Book Company, 1965, p. 151.

The Wilson home in Washington, D.C.

Our 28th President:

Woodrow Wilson

two terms

Tuesday, March 4, 1913

"There are a good many problems before the American people today and before me as president. But I expect to find the solution of these problems, just in the proportion that I am faithful in the study of the Word of God."[1]

Sunday, March 4, 1917

The Bible was opened to Psalm 119:11. "Your word have I hid in my heart, that I might not sin against Thee."[2]

With Mrs. Wilson standing on a chair to get a better view, Woodrow Wilson took his oath of office. After taking the oath, he stooped to kiss the opened Bible, held in the hands of James B. Moher, Deputy Clerk of the Supreme Court. The Bible was a little Bible belonging to Mrs. Wilson. After signing the flyleaf, the Bible was entrusted to Mrs. Wilson who "tucked it under her arm."[3]

The Bible, printed in Oxford by University Press, had been used at his Inauguration as Governor of New Jersey. It was used in both Inaugurations. In 1913, it was opened to Psalm 119. "Your word have I hid in my heart, that I might not sin against you" (v. 11).

Comment on the verse (Psalm 119:11) to which the Bible was opened:

If the Bible was opened "at random" as the *New York Times* article notes, it was most propitious that it should fall open at the 119th Psalm which is in praise of Holy Scripture. The son of a Presbyterian clergyman, Woodrow Wilson grew up on the Word of God in the Old and New Testaments. He once said: "The opinion of the Bible bred in me, not only by the teaching of my home,

60

when a boy, but also by every turn and experience of my life and every step of study, is that it is the one supreme source of the revelation of the meaning of life, the nature of God, and the spiritual nature and needs of men."

Monday, March 5, 1917

Mr. Wilson took the Bible in both hands and kissed it, his lips touching the words of Psalm 46. "God is our refuge and our strength, a very present help in the time of trouble." He closed the Bible and gave it to Mahler.[4]

Both Justice Edward O. White and Wilson signed their names to the oath which had been copied on the flyleaf of the Bible. Below Wilson's signature is the date, March 5, 1917. It is usually on exhibit at the Woodrow Wilson House, Washington, D.C., a property of the National Trust for Historic Preservation.

Comment on the verses (Psalm 46) to which the Bible was opened:

The 46th Psalm is one of the strongest expressions of faith to be found in the Bible. It speaks of not being afraid and expresses the assurance that God is with us "even if the seas roar and the earth is removed to the depths of the sea."

Woodrow Wilson had read this Psalm countless times. Perhaps he had heard his father preach on it. What a strong affirmation with which he began his second term!

1. *The New York Times,* March 5, 1917.
2. Presidential Inaugurations: Bibles and Scripture Passages, <http://memory.loc.gov/ammem/pihtml/pibible.html>.
3. Boller, Paul F., Jr., *Presidential Inaugurations* (Orlando, Florida: Harcourt, Inc., 2001), p. 27.
4. Kittler, Glenn D., *Hail To The Chief,* "The Inauguration Days Of Our Presidents," Philadelphia, Pennsylvania: Chilton Book Company, 1965, p. 159.

Ken Kettlewell and his daughter, Betsy, on the porch of the
Harding home in Marion, Ohio, from which Harding
conducted his "front porch" campaign for the presidency.

Our 29th President:
Warren G. Harding
one term

Friday, March 4, 1921

"I have always believed in the inspiration of the Holy Scriptures, whereby they have become the expression to men of the word and will of God. I believe that from every point of view, the study of the Bible is one of the most worthy to which men may devote themselves, and that in proportion as they know and understand it, their lives and actions are better." [1]

Mr. Harding requested permission to use the "George Washington Bible" as did Zachary Taylor, Dwight Eisenhower, Jimmy Carter, and George H. W. Bush.

The oath was administered by Chief Justice White, after which the new President kissed the Bible. [2] It was opened to Micah 6:8. [3] "What does the Lord require of you but to do justly, love mercy, and walk humbly with your God?"

Comment on the verse (Micah 6:8) to which the Bible was opened:

The prophet, Micah, asks a most significant question in this Bible verse. His very question would have us know that there are three things that the Lord requires of us in this life. Simply put, they are to work for justice, to show mercy to one another, and to walk humbly with God. We are called to more than a right belief. We are called to doing along with being. The "walking humbly" has to do with our being. The working for justice and the showing of mercy have to do with action. This president from Marion, Ohio, chose one of the most challenging verses in the Bible as he began his presidential administration.

1. American Bible Society, 1865 Broadway, New York, New York 10025.
2. Kittler, Glenn D., *Hail To The Chief,* "The Inauguration Days Of Our Presidents," Philadelphia, Pennsylvania: Chilton Book Company, 1965, p. 164.
3. Presidential Inaugurations: Bibles and Scripture Passages, <http://memory.loc.gov/ammem/pihtml/pibible.html>.

Our 30th President:

Calvin Coolidge

two terms

Friday, August 3, 1923

*"It is impossible to mentally or socially enslave a
Bible reading people. I am sorry for men who do
not read the Bible every day."*[1]

When word came of the death of President Harding, Vice-President Coolidge took the oath of office, becoming president, in his father's house in Plymouth, Vermont. His father was asleep in the old house of his ancestors which dated back to 1780. The house had no electricity and no indoor water facilities.

Mr. Coolidge was informed by telegram at midnight that President Harding had died. Colonel John Coolidge, 78, farmer and notary public, got out of bed, dressed, knelt by his bed to pray, and then went to the parlor to administer the oath of office to his son.

It was an old family Bible, published in New York by the American Bible Society. It is inscribed by President Coolidge, telling us that it lay on the table under his hand when he took the oath of office.[2]

Friday, March 4, 1925

The Bible, printed at Oxford by University Press, was given to him in boyhood by his grandmother. An inscription initialed by his wife attests to its use at the Inauguration. In 1969, both Bibles were in the possession of John Coolidge, Farmington, Connecticut.[3]

The oath was administered by former President, William H. Taft, who was Chief Justice after being President.

After taking the oath, the new President leaned over, his lips touching John 1:1. "In the beginning was the Word and the Word was with God and the Word was God."

65

Comment on the verse (John 1:1) to which the Bible was opened:

This verse had great meaning to Calvin Coolidge. His paternal grandfather, Calvin Galusha Coolidge, on his deathbed, asked Calvin to read the opening verses of John's Gospel. The elderly Galusha said he had read that same passage to *his* grandfather, from that same Bible.

With this verse, John opens his Gospel. He speaks of Jesus Christ as the Word, or the expression God uses to speak to us. He leads us to know that Jesus Christ did not just come into existence at Christmas time two thousand years ago. No, he was in the beginning with God. He is all the way back to the first verse of Genesis in the Old Testament. He was with God. Indeed, he was God.

A most interesting choice for President Coolidge to make!

1. Rare Book Library, Cathedral of Saint Peter and Saint Paul, Washington, D.C.
2. *Ibid.*
3. Boller, Paul F., Jr., *Presidential Inaugurations* (Orlando, Florida: Harcourt Inc., 2001), p. 119.

Our 31st President:

Herbert Hoover

one term

Monday, March 4, 1929

"As a nation, we are indebted to the Book of Books for our national ideals and representative institutions. Their preservation rests in adhering to its principles."[1]

Mr. Hoover had requested that the Bible be opened to Matthew 5, the Sermon on the Mount, but there was a slip up so it was opened to Proverbs 29:18, "Where there is no vision, the people perish."

The Bible had been for years in the possession of the Hoover family.[2] Its whereabouts is unknown.

Supreme Court Clerk Elmer Cropley handed Chief Justice Taft the Bible. Mr. Coolidge and Mr. Hoover were both sworn in by Mr. Taft, a former President. It was a small, new Oxford edition Bible. One of the hands of Chief Justice Taft also lay on the open Bible.

Comment on the verse (Proverbs 29:18) to which the Bible was opened:

In listing the qualities of leadership, the possessing of vision would rate at, or very near, the top. When people choose between two candidates for the highest office of the land, they must weigh carefully which one seems to have the clearer vision of what needs to be done and how best to do it.

This verse in the wisdom literature of the Bible rings loud and clear. Without vision, the people perish.

1. American Bible Society, 1865 Broadway, New York, New York 10025.
2. Rare Book Library, Cathedral of Saint Peter and Saint Paul, Washington, D.C.

Franklin Delano Roosevelt's home in
Hyde Park, New York

The gravesite of Franklin and Eleanor Roosevelt in the
rose garden of their home in Hyde Park, New York

Our 32nd President:

Franklin Delano Roosevelt

four terms

Saturday, March 4, 1933

*"The study of this book is a postgraduate course
in the richest library of human experience. There
is no other book so various as the Bible, nor one
so full of concentrated wisdom. Whether it be of
the law, business, morals, or that vision which
leads the imagination in the creation of
constructive enterprises for the happiness of
mankind, he who seeks for guidance in any of these
things may look inside its covers and find
illumination."*[1]

Used in the oath-taking was the Dutch Bible printed in
Dordecht about 1686. It had been in his family for three generations. The family had brought it over 300 years earlier. Leather
bound, it was printed in Dutch. It contained many vital Roosevelt
family statistics.[2]

If he omitted "So help me God," as some sources indicate,
perhaps it was because he was eager to outline his approach to the
economic crisis.

Chief Justice Charles Evans Hughes and FDR both placed their
hands on the Bible. It was opened to the thirteenth chapter of First
Corinthians, at his request He didn't kiss the Bible.[3]

Tuesday, January 20, 1937

With his palm on the old Dutch Bible of Clae Martenzen van Roosevelt, he took his oath of office as President for a second time. It was protected from the rain by a heavy sheet of cellophane. Again, it was opened to the New Testament passage, First Corinthians, chapter 13.[4]

Sunday, January 20, 1941

The Roosevelt Bible was open between the President and the Chief Justice. Again, it was opened to First Corinthians, chapter 13.

Saturday, January 20, 1945

Mr. Roosevelt went to service at a church before the Inauguration. In the service, the hymn the congregation sang was "O God Our Help in Ages Past."

As in previous inaugurations, three previous times as President, two as Governor of New York, again, the Bible was opened to First Corinthians, chapter 13, the "faith, hope, and love" chapter.

Comment on the passage (First Corinthians 13) to which the Bible was opened for all four of Mr. Roosevelt's inaugurations:

The thirteenth chapter of First Corinthians, written by the Apostle Paul, is one of the most beautiful and best loved chapters in the whole Bible. Speaking of the three great virtues, faith and hope and love, it is often quoted at weddings and on Mother's Day. Paul extols the greatness of faith. He goes on to speak of the great importance of hope. He concludes with the statement: "The greatest of these is love."

Franklin Delano Roosevelt chose a wonderful chapter for his four inaugurations.

1. Rare Book Library, Cathedral of Saint Peter and Saint Paul, Washington, D.C.
2. *Ibid.*
3. Kittler, Glenn D., *Hail To The Chief,* "The Inauguration Days Of Our Presidents," Philadelphia, Pennsylvania: Chilton Book Company, 1965, p. 181.
4. Presidential Inaugurations: Bibles and Scripture Passages, <http://memory.loc.gov/ammem/pihtml/pibible.html>.

Bronze statue of President Truman
Athens, Greece

Our 33rd President:

Harry S. Truman

a partial term and one full term

Thursday, April 12, 1945

"The fundamental basis of this nation's law was given to Moses on the Mount. The fundamental basis of our Bill of Rights comes from the teachings of Exodus and St. Matthew. I don't think we emphasize that enough these days. If we don't have the proper fundamental moral background, we will finally end up with a totalitarian government which does not believe in the right for anybody except the state." [1]

The ceremony was held in the Executive Wing of the White House. Mr. Truman was the first person to be sworn in with two Bibles, and the first whose ceremony was televised. Mr. Truman picked up the Bible that lay on the conference table as quick preparations were being made. It was a White House Bible, American Standard Version, published by Nelson in New York. It was used again in 1949.

The other Bible was a facsimile of the Gutenberg Bible issued in Leipzig in 1913. On the page where his left hand rested when he took the oath, an inscription declaring that it was the gift to Mr. Truman from the citizens of Jackson County, Missouri, his home county.

Both Bibles are in the Harry S. Truman Library in Independence, Missouri.

At 7:08 a.m., Bess and Margaret Truman having arrived, Chief Justice Harlan Fiske Stone was ready to administer the oath. Mr. Truman picked up the Bible that lay on the conference table and the oath was taken. [2]

Thursday, January 20, 1949

Chief Justice Vinson administered the oath. President Truman placed his left hand on the Bible. One Bible was opened to Matthew 5:3-11, the page where one finds the Beatitudes. The other was opened to Exodus 20:3-17, the Ten Commandments. After taking the oath, he bent quickly to kiss both Bibles. Then he turned to face the crowd.

Comment on the passage (Matthew 5:3-11) to which one Bible was opened:

Our Lord's Sermon on the Mount opens with these eight "Blesseds." Like a bell ringing, each one presents a spiritual truth as Jesus pronounces a blessing on "the poor in spirit ... the meek ... the merciful ..." Someone has said "the Beatitudes are the attitudes we ought to be at."

Comment on the passage (Exodus 20:3-17) to which the second Bible was opened:

In his own words quoted under the date of his inauguration, President Truman declares that the "fundamental basis of this nation's law was given to Moses on the Mount." One thinks of these words written by James Russell Lowell:

> *In vain we call old notions fudge,*
> *And bend our conscience to our dealing.*
> *The Ten Commandments will not budge,*
> *And stealing will continue stealing.*

1. American Bible Society, 1865 Broadway, New York, New York 10025.
2. Kittler, Glenn D., *Hail To The Chief,* "The Inauguration Days Of Our Presidents," Philadelphia, Pennsylvania: Chilton Book Company, 1965, p. 197.

Home of Dwight and Mamie Eisenhower
Gettysburg, Pennsylvania

Our 34th President:

Dwight David Eisenhower

two terms

Tuesday, January 20, 1953

"The Bible is endorsed by the ages. Our civilization is built upon its words. In no other book is there such a collection of inspired wisdom, reality, and hope." [1]

There were two Bibles there for the ceremony, as with President Truman. The first was the historic "George Washington Bible" opened to Psalm 127:1.

The other Bible, a gift of his mother, was one he had used as a cadet at West Point. [2] It was opened to Second Chronicles 7:14.

The new president offered a "private prayer," something none of his predecessors had ever done. He said: "My friends, before I begin the expression of those thoughts that I deem appropriate to this moment, would you permit me the privilege of uttering a little private prayer of my own?"

"Almighty God, as we stand here at this moment, my future associates in the executive branch of government join me in beseeching that Thou will make full and complete our dedication to the service of the people in this throng, and their fellow citizens everywhere. Give us, we pray, the power to discern clearly right from wrong, and allow all our words and actions to be governed thereby, and by the laws of this land. Especially we pray that our concern shall be for all the people, regardless of station, race, or calling. May cooperation be

76

*permitted and be the mutual aim of those who,
under the concepts of our Constitution, hold to
differing political faiths; so that all may work for
the good of our beloved country and Thy glory.
Amen."*

(I remember hearing President Eisenhower offer this fervent prayer. First Ohio Presbytery of the United Presbyterian Church of North America was holding its winter meeting in the First United Presbyterian Church, Dayton, Ohio, that day. We brought in a television so that we could all be a part of that historic event.)

Comment on the passages (Psalm 127:1 and 2 Chronicles 7:14) to which the Bibles were opened:
"Except the Lord build the house, they labor in vain that build it." This is one of the verses that I use at the opening of my wedding services. It is just right for the beginning of a marriage and the building of a home. It is just right for the beginning of a term as President.

> *"If my people ... will humble themselves, pray and
> seek my face, and turn from their wicked ways,
> then will I hear from heaven, forgive their sins and
> heal their land." Note the three things we the
> people* must *do, and then three things God* will *do
> for us. What a wonderful verse for the acceptance
> of the huge responsibility of President of the United
> States!*

Monday, January 21, 1957

The Inaugural date, January 20, 1957, fell on a Sunday. A small private ceremony was held that day. The public ceremony was postponed to Monday. Others had also taken their oaths twice when their date fell on a Sunday: Monroe, Taylor, Hayes, and Wilson.

Mr. Eisenhower's personal Bible was used, held open by Frank Sanderson, a White House aide. The Bible was opened to Psalm 33:12, "Blessed is that nation whose God is the Lord."[3] Chief Justice Earl Warren administered the oath.

Earlier that day, the presidential party went to the National Presbyterian Church where Dr. Edward Elson, the pastor, preached on the very verse the President had chosen for his open Bible.[4] Mr. Eisenhower had been baptized by Dr. Elson in that church. One can see in that church the low chair with a red velvet cushion, at which Mr. Eisenhower knelt for his baptism. That didn't take place until after his Inauguration. He explained that he waited until after becoming president so that it would not influence the citizens in their voting.

Comment on the passage (Psalm 33:12) to which the Bible was opened:

It is the earnest desire and prayer of all of us that the blessing of God might be upon our nation. How we need God's blessing! We may have intelligent, educated, wise leaders, but we humans, by ourselves, cannot, with our limitations, manage alone. We need God's help. If we serve the Lord, we will have that blessing. It must have been President Eisenhower's hope and prayer: that this nation would choose to serve the Lord and in serving the Lord, we would be blessed.

(On July 23, 1976, the bicentennial year of the signing of the Declaration of Independence, we dedicated "The Eisenhower Pew" in the First Presbyterian Church of Detroit where I was pastor. It marked the pew where Dwight Eisenhower had sat in worship on a September Sunday morning in 1952.)

1. National Bible Association, Comments about the Bible, Dwight D. Eisenhower.
2. Boller, Paul F., Jr., *Presidential Inaugurations* (Orlando, Florida: Harcourt, Inc., 2001), p. 25.
3. Rare Book Library, Cathedral of Saint Peter and Saint Paul, Washington, D.C.
4. Boller, Paul F., Jr., *Presidential Inaugurations* (Orlando, Florida: Harcourt, Inc., 2001), p. 29.

The riderless horse in President Kennedy's funeral procession
Washington, D.C.
Monday before Thanksgiving, November 25, 1963

The "eternal flame" at the tomb of President Kennedy
Arlington Cemetery, Virginia

Our 35th President:

John Fitzgerald Kennedy

one term

Saturday, January 21, 1961

"The Bible is a synthesis of that which abides and endures." [1]

In the Inaugural ceremony, the podium caught fire, caused by an electric motor used to adjust the lectern height. The motor had been used for years, but that day it had problems. Another problem: Robert A. Frost was sun-blinded as he read his poem, "The Gift Outright." He looked up and quoted the lines of the poem which he had written years earlier.

> *"The land was ours before we were the land's.*
> *She was our land more than a hundred years*
> *Before we were her people. She was ours*
> *In Massachusetts, in Virginia,*
> *But were England's, still colonials.*
> *Possessing what we were unpossessed by.*
> *Possessed by what we now no more possessed.*
> *Something we were withholding made us weak.*
> *Until we found out that it was ourselves*
> *We were withholding from our land of living,*
> *And forthwith found salvation in surrender.*
> *Such as we were we gave ourselves outright*
> *(The deed of gift was many deeds of war)*
> *To the land vaguely realizing westward*
> *But still unstoried, artless, unenhanced,*
> *Such as she was, such as she would become."*

Supreme Court Clerk James R. Browning held the closed family Douay Bible, an authorized Roman Catholic translation, which had belonged to Kennedy's Grandmother Fitzgerald. During the one-minute ceremony, Mr. Kennedy's hand moved from the Bible to his side. He was not actually touching the Bible as he took the oath. Some asked, "Is it valid for him to take the oath without his hand on the Bible?" The White House issued this statement: "The use of the Bible to solemnize the oath is merely traditional and not prescribed by the Constitution."[2]

1. American Bible Society, 1865 Broadway, New York, New York 10025.
2. Kittler, Glenn D., *Hail To The Chief,* "The Inauguration Days Of Our Presidents," Philadelphia, Pennsylvania: Chilton Book Company, 1965, p. 217.

Our 36th President:
Lyndon Baines Johnson

two terms

Friday, November 22, 1963

*"The Holy Bible was the most important possession
that our forbears placed aboard their ships as they
embarked for the New World."*[1]

On Air Force One in Dallas, Texas, following the death of John
F. Kennedy, the about-to-become President and his wife, along with
personal attendants, prepared for the oath-taking so the nation would
not be without a Commander-in-Chief. Mrs. Sarah T. Hughes, Federal District Judge, was ready to administer the oath. Crew member Sergeant Joseph Ayres remembered that President Kennedy had
kept a Bible by his bed, and he "fetched it."[2]

In *The Death Of The President,* William Manchester says that
the Bible belonged to President Kennedy who took it with him on
his travels. "It was an unusual copy, and very personal. The cover
was of tooled leather, the edges were hand-sewn; on the front there
was a gold cross, and on the inside cover, the tiny, sewn black-on-
black initials, JFK."

"Andrew Johnson had taken his oath of office in a Washington
hotel room; Chester A. Arthur in his Manhattan townhouse;
Theodore Roosevelt in a Buffalo home, Calvin Coolidge by
lamplight in the parlor of his father's Vermont farmhouse, and
Lyndon Baines Johnson in the sweltering cabin of an airplane....
Three minutes later, President Johnson issued his first order as the
Executive of the United States: 'Now let us be airborne.' "[3]

Wednesday, January 20, 1965

The Bible was closed for the Inauguration. It was published in Cleveland by the World Publishing Company and presented to Mr. Johnson and his wife upon their marriage in 1934. It had also been used when sworn in as Vice-President in 1961. In 1969, it was still in the possession of the Johnsons.

Holding the Bible, Lady Bird Johnson started a tradition followed by Pat Nixon, Rosalynn Carter, Nancy Reagan, Barbara Bush, Hilary Clinton and Laura Bush. It was a dog-eared family Bible. The photo shows that it was closed. As Chief Justice Warren started to read the oath, L.B.J. realized his hand was not on Bible, so he hurriedly placed it there.[4]

1. Lyndon Baines Johnson Library.
2. Kittler, Glenn D., *Hail To The Chief,* "The Inauguration Days Of Our Presidents," Philadelphia, Pennsylvania: Chilton Book Company, 1965, p. 223.
3. "The Torch Is Passed," *The Plain Dealer,* Cleveland, Ohio, pp. 22 and 23.
4. Boller, Paul F., Jr., *Presidential Inaugurations* (Orlando, Florida: Harcourt, Inc., 2001), p. 133.

Our 37th President:
Richard Milhous Nixon

two terms

Tuesday, January 21, 1969

"The Bible tells us that charity is the greatest virtue and that word 'charity' in the Bible is interpreted as love. It blesses both the giver and the receiver."[1]

"We acknowledge Thy divine help in the selection of our leadership every four years."
— Billy Graham's prayer in the ceremony

There were two Bibles, one published in 1938 and the other in 1873. Both had been in the Nixon family for many years, and had been used when Mr. Nixon was sworn in as Vice-President in 1953 and 1957. The Bibles were on a marble top table that was built for President Lincoln.[2]

One Bible was opened to Isaiah 2:4: "They shall beat their swords into plowshares and their spears into pruning hooks; nation shall not lift up sword against nation, neither shall they learn war anymore."[3]

Saturday, January 20, 1973

Two Bibles were there again, the same two as four years earlier. One was open to the same verse, Isaiah 2:4, as in 1969.[4]

85

Comment on the passage (Isaiah 2:4) to which the Bible was opened both times:

The prophet Isaiah gave us the picture of peace, when the instruments of war would be turned into instruments of peace. One thinks of the line in the Spiritual, "Ain't gonna study war no more." We were in the Vietnam conflict at the time, and this was a well-chosen passage for Mr. Nixon's inaugurations, or for any President's Inauguration at any time. We hope and pray that our nation never loses sight of this image from the prophet.

1. Cummings, Greg, The Nixon Library and Birthplace.
2. Rare Book Library, Cathedral of Saint Peter and Saint Paul, Washington, D.C.
3. List compiled by the Clerk of the Supreme Court, 1938.
4. Presidential Inaugurations: Bibles and Scripture Passages,<http://memory.loc.gov/ammem/pihtml/pibible.html>.

President Ford's office
Grand Rapids, Michigan

Our 38th President:

Gerald R. Ford

one term

Friday, August 9, 1974

"In my own life and throughout my career in public service, I have found in the pages of the Bible a steady compass and a source of great strength and peace."[1]

The Bible used in the inauguration ceremony was a gift from Ford's oldest son, Michael, a student at Gordon Cromwell Seminary, South Hamilton, Massachusetts. It had been used when he was sworn as Vice-President eight months earlier.[2]

Mr. Ford placed his hand on the Bible held by his wife, Betty. It was opened to Proverbs 3:5-6. "Trust in the Lord with all thy heart and lean not unto your own understanding. In all thy ways acknowledge Him, and He will direct your paths." These verses are the prayer which Mr. Ford used each night.[3]

The ceremony was held in the East Room of White House. Chief Justice Warren Burger administered the oath.

Comment on the verses (Proverbs 3:5-6) to which the Bible was opened:

In the wisdom literature of the Bible, the book of Proverbs presents divine wisdom and truth. Our part is to trust in the Lord and not depend entirely upon our own *limited* understanding. If we acknowledge the Lord in all our decision making, the Lord will direct us in the right way. This is a most worthy word of counsel to any president or any individual who wants to make the right decisions in life.

1. American Bible Society, 1865 Broadway, New York, New York 10025
2. Rare Book Library, Cathedral of Saint Peter and Saint Paul, Washington, D.C.
3. Boller, Paul F., Jr., *Presidential Inaugurations* (Orlando, Florida: Harcourt, Inc., 2001), p. 123.

Our 39th President:

Jimmy Carter

one term

Friday, January 21, 1977

"The Bible has been a major source of teaching and reinforcing the values of many of our people throughout our history." [1]

While his wife, Rosalyn, held the family Bible, Mr. Carter placed his left hand on it. Also there for the ceremony was the "George Washington Bible," which was used in the Inauguration of our first President in 1789. [2]

The Bible was opened to an Old Testament passage, Micah 6:8. "What does the Lord require of you but to do justly, love mercy, and to walk humbly with your God?" [3] (President Harding's inaugural Bible was also opened to this passage.)

An active member of the Baptist Church in Plains, Georgia, Mr. Carter often taught a Sunday school class, even after he became President. He had done missionary work in the Northeast earlier in his life and witnessed to the President of South Korea, a Buddhist, encouraging him to become a Christian. His daily custom was to read the Bible and pray. [4]

Comment on the passage (Micah 6:8) to which the Bible was opened:

The prophet Micah asks the question of each of us and all of us, and we cannot dodge the implications of each point. Micah says the Lord "requires" these things of us: to do justly, to love mercy, and to walk humbly with our God.

The choice was carefully made. Carter had probably read and pondered this passage often. It was a good choice for him, or for any one at any time throughout life.

1. American Bible Society, 1865 Broadway, New York, New York 10025.
2. Boller, Paul F., Jr., *Presidential Inaugurations* (Orlando, Florida: Harcourt, Inc., 2001), p. 132.
3. Presidential Inaugurations: Bibles and Scripture Passages, <http://memory.loc.gov/ammem/pihtml/pibible.html>.
4. Boller, Paul F., Jr., *Presidential Anecdotes,* p. 342.

A "Reagan For President" poster
1980 Republican Convention
Detroit, Michigan

Our 40th President:
Ronald Wilson Reagan

two terms

Wednesday, January 21, 1981

"Within the covers of the Bible are all the answers for all the problems we face. The Bible can touch the heart, order minds, and refresh souls."[1]

Both Mr. Reagan and Mr. Eisenhower chose Second Chronicles 7:14 for the open page in the Bible on which they placed their left hand. "If my people, who are called by my name, will humble themselves, pray and seek my face, and turn from their wicked ways, then will I hear from heaven, will forgive their sin, and will heal the land."[2]

The oath was taken on a family Bible much used by his late mother, Nellie Reagan. She often read verses from that Bible in her "jail ministry" in Dixon, Illinois. The Bible had been bandaged with tape so that it could continue to be used. It had been in the family for many decades. Inside the back cover were names and dates of births, marriages, and deaths in the Wilson ancestry of the Reagan family. Deeply moved, Mrs. Reagan held the Bible while her husband's left hand rested on the sacred page.

Inside the front cover of the King James Bible was a sonnet composed by Nancy Reagan dedicating her life to "higher, nobler things." The first line is a paraphrase of John Milton's famous poem, "On His Blindness."[3]

> *When I consider how my life is spent*
> *The most that I can do will be to prove*
> *'Tis by his side, each day, to move,*
> *to higher, nobler things my mind is bent.*
> *Thus giving of my strength, which God has lent*
> *I strive some needy soul's unrest, to soothe.*

Lest they the paths of righteousness shall lose.
Through fault of mine, my Maker to present
If I should fail to show them of their needs
How would I hope to meet him face to face,
or give a just account of all my ways?
In thought of mind, in word, and in each deed

My life must prove the power of grace
By every action through my living days.

Monday, January 21, 1985

Mr. Reagan took his oath privately on Sunday, January 20. Due to below zero temperatures, the Inaugural Committee recommended canceling the expected parade the next day, and the ceremony was held in the Capitol Rotunda. The same Bible was used as in the first Inaugural, and it was opened again to the same passage, Second Chronicles 7:14.

At the California burial of President Reagan on June 11, 2004, the Rev. Michael Wenning quoted the Second Chronicles 7:14 verse.

Comment on the verses (Second Chronicles 7:14) to which the Bible was opened:

The text makes it quite plain that if we fulfill certain requirements, God will bless us. The requirements are three: to humble ourselves, to pray, and to turn from our wicked ways. Three blessings follow: God will hear our prayer, will forgive our sin, and will heal our land.

Great choice for Mr. Reagan, or for any president, or for any of us!

1. National Bible Association, Comments about the Bible, Ronald Reagan.
2. Presidential Inaugurations: Bibles and Scripture Passages, <http://memory.loc.gov/ammem/pihtml/pibible.html>.
3. *New York Times,* January 21, 1981, p. 191.

Our 41st President:

George Herbert Walker Bush

one term

Saturday, January 21, 1989

There were two Bibles chosen for the Inauguration ceremony. The family Bible was opened to the Beatitudes of Jesus in the Sermon on the Mount, Matthew 5:[1]

"Blessed are the poor in spirit, for theirs is the Kingdom of Heaven.

Blessed are they that mourn, for they shall be comforted.

Blessed are the meek, for they shall inherit the earth.

Blessed are they that hunger and thirst after righteousness, for they shall be filled.

Blessed are the merciful, for they shall obtain mercy.

Blessed are the pure in heart, for they shall see God.

Blessed are peacemakers, for they shall be called the children of God.

Blessed are they who are persecuted for righteousness' sake, for theirs is the Kingdom of Heaven."

The family Bible was held by Barbara Bush. The "George Washington Bible" was below the family Bible, opened at random.

Comment on the passage (Matthew 5) to which the Bible was opened:

The Sermon on the Mount opens with the Beatitudes all of which begin with the word "Blessed." Jesus pronounces a blessing upon one group after another. Sometimes we find ourselves among the "poor in spirit." Other times we will be among the mourners ... the merciful ... the peacemakers. This passage has been called "The Heavenly Octave," because it strikes eight notes which remind us of the eight notes in the musical scale.

---

1. Presidential Inaugurations: Bibles and Scripture Passages
   <http://memory.loc.gov/ammem/pihtml/pibible.html>.

Our 42nd President:

William Jefferson Clinton

two terms

Thursday, January 21, 1993

"I encourage my fellow Americans to read the Bible often and carefully. In doing so, each of us — and our country — will find resources for today and will secure hope for tomorrow."[1]

Mr. Clinton took his oath of office with his hand resting on an open page in his grandmother's Bible, that Bible being a gift to him when he was the Governor of Arkansas. It was the King James version, and it was opened to Galatians 6:8. "He that soweth to his own flesh shall of the flesh reap corruption but he that soweth to the spirit shall of the spirit reap eternal life." This was a verse he often quoted in speeches.[2]

Hilary Clinton, wife of the new President, held the Bible, continuing a custom which Lady Bird Johnson had started.

Making his eighth appearance at a Presidential Inauguration, Billy Graham prayed. The famous evangelist has participated in more Inaugurals than Chief Justice Tanney, but fewer than Chief Justice Marshall.

The Bible used in the ceremony was on display at the Washington National Cathedral for several months after the Inauguration, in an exhibit titled, "So Help Me God."

Comment on the verse (Galatians 6:8) to which the Bible was opened:

In this passage, the Apostle Paul speaks of our two natures: the spiritual and the physical. Tempted constantly to enjoy the things of the body, Paul makes it clear that we reap eternal life when we "sow to the spirit."

Interesting passage for a president to choose for his inauguration! In his inaugural address, Mr. Clinton quoted an earlier verse in the same paragraph: "Be not weary in well doing, for in due season you shall reap if you faint not."

Monday, January 20, 1997

The Bible used in the 1993 Inauguration was used again. This time, it was open to an Old Testament passage, Isaiah 58:12. "Thou shalt raise up the foundations of many generations, and thou shalt be called the repairer of the breach, the restorer of paths to dwell in."

Richard Penedetto's wrote in his column: "Our President has charted a difficult path for himself. Whether he can navigate it successfully will be in part up to him, in part up to us, and in part up to the course of national and world events over which he or we have little control."[3]

Comment on the verse (Isaiah 58:12) to which the Bible was opened:

The Old Testament prophet, Isaiah, holds out the challenge and hope that one can become a "repairer" and a "restorer." It would seem that Mr. Clinton had the deep desire that these two titles might describe his work as President.

1. American Bible Society, 1865 Broadway, New York, New York 10025.
2. Shannon, Margaret, curator of an exhibit, "Presidential Religion," National Cathedral Associated Press L 19-97.
3. *USA Today*, January 20, 1997.

Our 43rd President:

George W. Bush

current President

Saturday, January 20, 2001

"I read the Bible regularly. I read through the 'One Year Bible' every other year. During the years between, I pick different chapters at different times."[1]

Laura Bush, wife of the new President, held a closed family Bible as Mr. Bush placed his hand on it and took his oath as the new President of the United States of America.

But had not the "George Washington Bible" been brought from New York for the event attended by a committee of three from Saint John's Lodge No. 1? Yes, and it had arrived on time a day early, at 2:59 p.m. A small contingent of Freemasons dressed in colonial military garb met the officials who had brought it from New York. All was ready for this Bible to play a part in its sixth presidential inauguration, but alas, rain! The New York committee decided not to have it in the ceremony.

For several days prior to the Inauguration, the significance of the "George Washington Bible" caught the attention of both the broadcast and the print media. It had been used by the new President's father in his 1989 Inauguration.

In her column the day before the inauguration, Emily Gest wrote: "The Bible used to swear in the first George will be used to swear in the 43rd President, George W. Bush." She also wrote: "The Masons offer their Bible for every inauguration ... it is so fragile that even Supreme Court Justice William Rehnquist will not be allowed to touch it. Instead, it will rest on a red cushion trimmed in gold braid that Rehnquist will hold."[2] (The columnist's prediction did not come to pass.)

1. American Bible Society, 1865 Broadway, New York, New York 10025.
2. Gest, Emily, *New York Daily News,* January 19, 2001.

The flag of the United States of America
flying over the U.S.S. Arizona Memorial
Pearl Harbor, Hawaii

Bibliography

American Bible Society, 1865 Broadway, New York, New York 10025

"Bible And Scripture Passages Used By Presidents In Taking The Oath Of Office," Internet: Architect of the Capitol

Boller, Paul F., Jr., *Presidential Anecdotes,* New York: Oxford University Press, 1965

Boller, Paul F., Jr., *Presidential Inaugurations,* San Diego: A Harvest Book Harcourt, Inc., 2001

Cambridge Jeffersonian, December 8, 2000 (Cambridge, Ohio)

Halley, Henry H., *Bible Handbook,* Grand Rapids, Michigan: Zondervan, 1962

Kittler, Glenn D., *Hail to the Chief,* "The Inauguration Days of Our Presidents," Philadelphia, Pennsylvania: Chilton Book Company, 1965

Internet: National Bible Association, non-profit educational association incorporated in the state of New York, founded in 1940

Rare Book Library, Cathedral of Saint Peter and Saint Paul, Washington, D.C.

The Plain Dealer, "The Torch Is Passed," Cleveland, Ohio

"The Death of a President," Associated Press, Western Printing and Litghography Company

Wright, John, *Historic Bibles In America,* New York: T. Whittaker, 1905

Appendix

In 1934, as a boy in the Junior Department in the Sunday school of the College Drive United Presbyterian Church in New Concord, Ohio, I learned this alphabet of Bible verses, one verse each week for 26 weeks. Mrs. Howard Geyer was the Superintendent who encouraged us to do this.

An Alphabet Of Bible Verses

"A soft answer turns away wrath, but grievous words stir up anger." — Proverbs 15:1

"Be not overcome of evil, but overcome evil with good." — Romans 12:21

"Cast your burden on the Lord, and He will sustain you." — Psalm 55:22

"Depart from evil and do good; seek peace and pursue it." — Psalm 34:14

"Enter ye in at the straight gate; for wide is the gate that leads to destruction." — Matthew 7:13

"...For I know whom I have believed, and am persuaded that he is able to keep that which I have committed unto him against that day." — 2 Timothy 1:12

"Go therefore and make disciples of all the nations...." — Matthew 28:19

"Herein is my Father glorified, that you bear much fruit...." — John 15:8

"I am the good shepherd; the good shepherd gives His life for His sheep." — John 10:11

"You shall love the Lord your God with all your heart, and with all your soul, and with all your mind, and with all your strength." — Mark 12:30

"Keep thy heart with all diligence, for out of it are the issues of life." — Proverbs 4:23

"Let your light shine before others, so that they may see your good works and give glory to your Father in heaven." — Matthew 5:16

"My help comes from the Lord, who made heaven and earth." — Psalm 121:2

"Now is the accepted time; now and today is the day of salvation." — 2 Corinthians 6:2

"O taste and see that the Lord is good; blessed is the man who trusteth in him." — Psalm 34:8

"Pride goeth before destruction, and a haughty spirit before a fall." — Proverbs 16:18

"Quicken thou me according to thy word." — Psalm 119:25

"Remember the Sabbath day, to keep it holy." — Exodus 20:8

"Set a watch, O Lord, before my mouth...." — Psalm 141:3

"The Lord is my shepherd..." — Psalm 23:1

"Understanding is a well spring of life to him who hath it."   — Proverbs 16:22

"...Verily, verily, I say unto thee, except a man be born again, he cannot see the kingdom of God."   — John 3:3

"Examine me, O Lord, and prove me; try my reins and my heart."   — Psalm 26:2

"You are the light of the world. A city built on a hill cannot be hid."   — Matthew 5:14

"...Zaccheus, make haste, and come down; for today I must abide at thy house."   — Luke 19:5

The Author

Kenneth V. Kettlewell was born in New Concord, Ohio, in 1925. He attended the public schools there and went on to graduate from Muskingum College in his hometown. Earning a theological degree from Pittsburgh Theological Seminary, he became a Presbyterian minister, serving churches in Ohio, Pennsylvania, and Michigan. He earned a Doctor of Ministry degree from McCormick Theological Seminary in Chicago. He received an honorary Doctor of Divinity degree from Muskingum College.

He and his wife, Jean, have celebrated their 57th wedding anniversary. Parents of three children and nine grandchildren, they are retired and living in the Ohio Masonic Retirement Village in Springfield, Ohio.